Game Days

Game Days

Edited by Chris Dorsey

WILLOW CREEK PRESS

MINOCQUA, WISCONSIN

Text and photography credits appear on pages 7-8.

ISBN 1-57223-013-4

Published by WILLOW CREEK PRESS
an imprint of Outlook Publishing
P.O. Box 881
Minocqua, WI 54548

For information on other Willow Creek titles, write or call
1-800-850-WILD.

Printed in the U.S.A.

Library of Congress Cataloging-in-Publication Data

Game days : a tribute to North American big game hunting /
  edited by Chris Dorsey.
      p.   cm.
    ISBN 1-57223-013-4
    1. Big game hunting—North America. 2. Big game
animals—North America. 3. Big game hunting—North
America—Pictorial works. 4. Big game animals—North
America—Pictorial works.   I. Dorsey, Chris, 1965-   .
SK40.G36   1994
799.2'6'097—dc20   94-35383
                                                  CIP

The Photographers

Alan and Sandy Carey, pages 4, 12, 18, 32-33, 41, 43, 107, 111, 143, 169, 173, 176.

Bill Kinney, pages 5, 137, 149.

Lon E. Lauber, pages 6, 7, 79, 113, 123, 155, 165.

Denver A. Bryan, pages 8, 45, 126.

Tim Christie, pages 9, 53, 71, 81, 84, 95, 115, 121.

Bill McRae, pages 11, 55, 83, 92-93.

Erwin and Peggy Bauer, pages 16-17, 51, 61, 97, 101, 117, 147, 152-153, 157, 159, 171.

Charles Alsheimer, pages 25, 47, 141, 145.

Judd Cooney, pages 35, 63, 103.

Ron Spomer, pages 37, 39, 59, 73, 109, 119, 125, 162.

Neal and Mary Jane Mishler, pages 49, 75.

Bill Vaznis, pages 57, 65.

Chris Dorsey, pages 67, 73.

Michael H. Francis, pages 69, 99, 139, 151, 175.

Leonard Lee Rue III, page 77.

Mark Kayser, pages 105, 161.

The Writers

Robert F. Jones, page 19, "God Bless the Running Deer" *Game Journal* Vol 1:5.

Walter E. Howard, page 34, from *Animal Rights vs. Nature*.

Ralph Waldo Emerson, page 36.

Norm Strung, page 38, from "Home Is the Hunter," *Game Country* December 1988, pg. 34.

Norm and Sil Strung, page 122, from "Camp Meat," *Game Country* August 1989, pg. 5.

Theodore Roosevelt, pages 40, 146, 154, 164, from *The Wilderness Reader*. The New American Library; and pages 62, 98, 160, from *Ranch Life and the Hunting Trail*, 1896.

Tom Brown, page 42, from *The Tracker*, Putnam Publishing Group.

Meriwether Lewis, page 44, from *The Journals of Lewis and Clark*.

Barry Lopez, page 46, "The Moment of Encounter," *Parabola: the Magazine of Myth and Tradition* Vol.XVI, No. 2 (Summer 1991) pg. 56; and pages 82, 142, from *Arctic Dreams* by Barry Lopez. Reprinted by permission of Sterling Lord Literistic, Inc. Copyright © by Barry Lopez.

Thomas McIntyre, page 48, "Racks" and page 110 "Goat" from *Dreaming the Lion*, Countrysport Press, Traverse City, MI.

Oliver Wendell Holmes, page 50.

Frederic Remington, page 52, "Bear Chasing in the Rocky Mountains" from *Great Bear Adventures*, Key-Porter Publishers.

Roderick Haig-Brown, page 54, from *Measure of the Year,* Lyons and Burford Publishers, 1950.

Robert Ruark, page 56, 112, from *The Old Man and the Boy*, 1957; and page 58, from *Horn of the Hunter,* Safari Press/Woodbine Pub. Co.

Patrick Stephens, page 60, from "A Rocky Mountain High"

Tom Walker, pages 64, 124, 140, from *Shadows on the Tundra*, Stackpole Books.

Johnathon L. Morgan, page 66, from "Life Is a Current"

Jose Ortega y Gasset, page 68, reprinted with permission of Charles Scribner's Sons, an imprint of Macmillan Publishing, from *Meditations on Hunting* by Jose Ortega y Gasset. © 1972, 1985 Revista de Occidente S/A.

Guy De La Valdene, page 70, from *Making Game,* Clark City Press.

Aldo Leopold, pages 72, 114, from *A Sand County Almanac,* Oxford University Press.

Aaron Fraser Pass, page 74, from "Trails and Tails"; page 80, from "Above and Beyond"; pages 102, 118, from "Rams of the North Slope"; and page 174, from "Of Elk and Elephants"

Michael McGurty, page 76, from "Dining Out"

Gerald Cummings, page 78, from "Rolling Stones and Other Calibers"

Lionel Atwill, page 85, "The Fourth Day"

Jack O'Connor, page 94, from *Outdoor Life* March 1960; pages 106, 170, from *The Best of Jack O'Connor,* and page 136, from *Game in the Desert Revisited,* both books published by Amwell Press, P.O. Box 5385, Clinton, NJ 08809.

Seth Thorsen, page 96, from "Lichen Hooves and Barren Land"; and page 100, from "Lichen Hooves and Barren Land"

Caspar Whitney, page 104.

Saxton Pope, page 108.

Jim Fergus, pages 116, 138, from *The Hunter's Road* by Jim Fergus, Henry Holt and Company, Inc.

Alonson Skinner, page 120, from "Bear Customs of the Cree," circa 1914, *Great Bear Adventures,* Key-Porter Publishers.

Thomas McGuane, page 127, "The Heart of the Game" from *An Outside Chance*, published by Houghton-Mifflin, 1977.

Trebbe Johnson, page 144, from "Wilderness and Hearth: The Cycle of the Hunt," *Parabola* Summer 1991, pg. 79.

Robert Frost, page 148, from "The Road Not Taken," 1916.

Joseph Campbell, page 150, from *The Power of Myth*, Doubleday and Co., New York.

Ted Kerasote, page 156, from *Bloodties*, Random House, Inc.

Don Robertson, page 158, from "Tundraiffic!"

Matthew B. Connolly, Jr., page 162, from "Why I Hunt," *Ducks Unlimited* December, 1990.

Thomas Roberts, page 166, from "True North"

Archibald Rutledge, page 168, from *An American Hunter,* 1937.

Dwight Schuh, page 172, from "Elk Hunting Runs Deep," *Game Country* October 1989.

DEDICATION

For brother Joseph, my first and favorite hunting partner.

ACKNOWLEDGEMENTS

In the process of mining for editorial gold, I encountered countless more nuggets than could be collected here. The book before you was four years in the making, representing a gradual sifting process that rendered a distillate of insightful prose. Many works have already withstood the harsh winds of time and literary criticism, others are the achievements of contemporary authors who have made their own inroads into the world of timeless sporting literature. The marriage of pen and pictures was made possible by the extraordinary works of some of America's most talented wildlife photographers. I count myself a fan of one and all.

INTRODUCTION

By Chris Dorsey

Capturing the essence of the hunt and the hunter is like bottling a cloud, for the definition is as elusive and varied as the game we pursue. However, like the quest for a mythical trophy, a beast of unfathomable proportions, we cannot resist such temptation. It is that search, that stalk through the game fields of our memories and imagination that has been the genesis of *Game Days*.

To hunt big game is to awaken the senses from the dormancy brought about by an overdose of civilization, to see without the filter of urbania that sometimes surrounds us and too often swallows us. A walk in game country is an escape from domestication, a fork in the path between that which brings meaning to life and that which is meant to be life. We yearn to flee the egg-factory high-rises of the gateless pens that we call cities, to stalk the realms of wildness and shed the mundane in an effort to grab life in its grandest state.

Part of the lure to any stay in game country is the camp and the cast of characters that make each one special. As dramatic as the vistas might be, as enchanting as the quest for game can be, we carry the memories of old friends with us to hunting camps whenever we step from the malaise of modern life to the narcotic of wild country. Indeed, to share time in game country with a friend who knows why you hunt, and who shares your reverence for it, is one of life's elemental pleasures. Communication in a camp of kindred spirits is more a matter of what isn't said than what is.

At the center of any camp is the campfire, the natural phenomenon that warms conversations and thaws the hyper-tension that has become the by-product of modern society. Campfires are the hunter's hearth, the central image of a timeless work of art, a unifying theme that holds an age-old drama together. What each of us sees as we stare into the flames is a reflection of other campfires and other times, different places where the same magical mood of the hunt was found.

The vast stage that is home to the continent's great beasts is both mesmerizing and inspiring. The mountains of the West are the enemy of civilization, but the blessing of civilization's inhabitants. The higher a hunter climbs, the closer he is to heaven. The peaks and valleys of big game country serve as a metaphor for the hunter, reminding us of the challenges and rewards that we stalk as we travel the hunter's path. When one has tasted the wild, untrammeled natural theaters, the thirsting for more is the answering of a racial beckoning that has echoed through man's genetic code for a millennium.

You'll know you're in big game country when you're alone with your thoughts, free to survive on your vigor and wits, the same two traits that kept paleolithic and neolithic man from becoming prey. You'll find more than game in the best of our big game lands, you'll find intrigue as you look around a sprawling valley punctuated by ivory peaks, and a smile will grow across your face as you become distracted from the talk of others but focused in your own thoughts.

Hunting big game is about open space, about breaking from community and socialization to taste the frontier spirit that first pushed our forefathers to the edge of one continent and then to the wilderness of another. Game country and wilderness are often the same: places where you can find yourself as well as game. Time in game country is measured by sun and stars. It's a place where thoughts are flavored by the generous muses of wildness, the same inspiration that guided the pens of the authors whose thoughts are herein contained.

It is the animals, the protagonists of the epic story of the hunt, that draw us to the fertile lands of game country. Whether whitetails in the river bottoms or mountain goats on the cliffs, our big game are the players in a geologic chess game that stimulates every sense. The animals are, in their mysterious lives, riddles whose tracks leave us clues to the great question that is the stalk, that is life itself.

One looks with wonder at the massive herds of caribou

that draw life from lichen that draw life from rock that first surfaced with the birth of the planet. It seems impossible that such large forms can be sustained from such spartan environs. To find caribou, follow the tracks of the glacier that are the telltale lakes of the far north. If you get lost, let the heavenly dance of the Northern Lights be your guide. Caribou are much like hunters, forever suffering from wanderlust. They're the vagabond voyageurs of the arctic, undulating through time in an endless migration.

Following North America's last great game herds is the grizzly, one of the few remaining mammals to challenge our position in the food chain. A grizzly isn't so much an animal as it is a presence, like the whisper of wind through spruce. When we walk in land ruled by the beasts, they live in our psyche, following us like a shadow in our thoughts. Whose pulse doesn't rise in grizzly country when the snap of a twig triggers evolutionary messages through one's nerves? Who that has walked in the land of the grizzly hasn't, at least for one nightmarish instant, thought of a close encounter with one of the malevolent beasts?

Leave the forests, climb above the meadows, and you'll find yourself eye-to-eye with the sheep, the noble guardians of the slopes. It's a place where wind and scree meet in an endless struggle for survival. Perched above the sheep, however, are the goats, lords of the crags. To most, mountain goats are little more than distant spots of chalk on the otherwise slate gray escarpments of the West. Before you can stalk them, you must first be able to walk in the clouds.

There are so many more: The moose, that lumbering billboard of tenacity. The pronghorn, the prairie darter. Who could forget the black bear, the shadow of the woods. What about elk, the animal that whistles the hunter's favorite tune. Then there are the deer, the king whitetail and the mule deer, the prince of the highlands. The difference between a yearling mule deer buck and a monarch of the mountains is the difference between ignorance and sophistication, a pre-schooler and a graduate, a pitcher's mound and Pike's Peak.

None, however, have commanded the following that the whitetail has. Its adaptability is matched only by its durability. Statistically speaking, a record-book whitetail is the hardest of all creatures to find. Your chances of subduing one are something akin to happening upon a unicorn or snagging the Loch Ness monster. For the average whitetail hunter in search of a record book entry, a hunting license is little more than a lottery ticket. Nonetheless, it's a ticket coveted by all.

The heritage of the hunter is a rich one, laced with tales of discovery and adventure. What would you trade to walk— if only for a day—beside Lewis and Clark, to ponder the immense bison herds floating across an endless sea of blue-stem? Imagine the first encounter with a grizzly in the dark recesses of a northern forest. While our ancestors hunted to live, we now live to hunt. Our passion for the hunt, the country, and the game is found in the habitat of these pages; so many tributes to the events we call *Game Days*.

GOD BLESS THE RUNNING DEER

By Robert F. Jones

Four thirty in the morning. Black and cold, with the wind filling to the north in fitful gusts. A crease of pre-dawn light traces the shoulder of Bear Mountain to the east, sharp with spikes of spruce, scrub oak, cut-over beech, and popple, as if some drunken draftsman with the shakes had run a grease pencil up the sky. I stand wool-clad but shivering outside the deer camp, awaiting a portent. It's opening day.

Inside, Dick Raymond is busy as usual at the kitchen stove, cackling like Woody Woodpecker as he prepares breakfast—eggs, bacon, thick slabs of fried ham, with sides of pickled onions, home fries, grated garlic and a pot of Dick's own home-grown horseradish guaranteed to make a strong man cry Mama. It goes good on eggs. Warm, yellow lamplight fills the room, gilding the tines of antlers on the wall, and logs in the fireplace pop and flare like ghostly gunshots. Tousled, unshaven men stagger fragile as fever victims in longjohns and boots toward the coffee pot, hoping to re-glue their nervous systems. The poker game didn't break up until midnight.

Deer hunters always vow, before the season starts, that this year they'll play it smart. No booze, no poker game, get to bed sensibly early this time—nine p.m. Well, maybe ten. Or ten-thirty? Okay, maybe a couple of hands of five-card draw. High-low, of course. Wild cards? Sure, maybe a few. Might as well play seven card stud for the last hand, don't you think? We won't be able to sleep right away anyway, so maybe a beer just before bedtime. A Seven & Seven did you say? You're right—drink a beer before going to bed, you'll be up at two in the morning to drain it off. I might as well join you—yeah, Jack will be fine, no water. Oh, is it my deal already? All right, this game's called Spit-in-the-Ocean . . .

Dawn of Opening Day is fraught with hope and ruin. The hope rises slowly out of the ruin of the deer hunter. That big buck will be there this year, for sure. Up by the Bear's Den, perhaps. Or maybe near the Split Rock. Spruce Peak? Burnt Ridge? Or over Bass Hill toward the Oven. Maybe Little Haystack, with the wind out of the north the way it is . . . I need an omen, a portent, some heavenly sign to point me in the right direction.

And then it comes. From the camps farther off in the woods I hear a low coughing growl, then another, then a cacophony of rumbling, snarling, belching, roaring engines. Headlight beams pierce the darkness like frayed white fingers. It sounds for a moment like a mini-Indy 500 out there in the gloom— "Gentlemen, start your engines!" Here they come, nose to tail, hunters mounted on mud-spattered three- and four-wheeler all-terrain cycles, the latest bane to the ancient and once-honorable sport of deer hunting—four, five, no six of them in a pack, the hunters hunched over their handlebars, rifles slung across their backs, bulky in their red and green and orange checked coats, mittened hands screwing freely at throttles, their faces corpse white in the dancing, reflected glare of their headlamps. The whole hellish pack of them turns right, up the Fourth-of-July Road. That decides it for me. Today I'll hunt in the opposite direction—up Bass Hill, into the Oven.

The door of the deer camp opens. A sprightly figure emerges and hikes purposely toward the outhouse, where Dick Raymond, whose camp this is, has generously, nay, thoughtfully covered the toilet seat with a fur slipcover. The man headed in that direction is none other than my close friend and co-worker, Bill Eppridge, whose job it is this day to capture on film the ineffable essence, tradition, lore, and ritual of that great American event, The Opening Day of Deer Season. Epp pauses as he passes me, and turns so that his face is bathed in the yellow light from the window. He cocks his head sideways and grins devilishly, then begins to sing me a tum-ti-dum ditty of his own composition:

If you go out in the woods today
You're in for a big surprise
'Cause someone's gonna put a bullet
Right between your eyes.

I chuckle halfheartedly, Eppridge launches blithely into the refrain:

They bound, they bound, they leap all around,
They run until they're finally downed;
Today's the day of the Deer Hunter's Killing Orgy . . .

Thanks a lot, old buddy. There are doubts enough working already in the hearts and minds of most deer hunters on Opening Day—from the changeability of wind and weather to the accuracy of one's rifle (no matter how many rounds you've fired while sighting it in)—without having to worry about getting plugged. For all the doubts and dubious hazards, though, some 12 million Americans (most of them men) take to the woods each autumn, gun in hand, to seek a confrontation with North America's premier big game animal: the wily white-tailed deer. According to the U.S. Fish & Wildlife Service, there are about 20,000,000 white-tailed deer in the U.S. today. Since only one hunter in ten will actually succeed in killing a deer, the main question in each hopeful Nimrod's mind on the morning of Opening Day is if he will be one of the fortunate gunners. Though the figure varies from state to state and season to season, anywhere from a quarter to half of all the deer killed will be shot between sun-up and noon on Opening Day morning.

But Opening Day is important for more than the imminent prospects of success or, more likely, frustration and failure. Over the years, since game seasons were first imposed in this country in the 18th Century, Opening Day of Deer Season has acquired an almost mystical aura. To the inveterate deer hunter, it is not unlike Christmas, New Year's, Thanksgiving, or even his own birthday—all rolled into one,

and nicely spiced with gunpowder. Indeed, some men—myself included—measure the years from deer season to deer season. (I also measure them from trout season to trout season, and from bird season to bird season, which gives me the bonus of three "Happy New Years" per annum, one of the unsung blessings of being an outdoorsman.)

Communities too look forward eagerly to Opening Day. In many regions, schools close during the first week of deer season. Stores and whole shopping malls hold special sales for "deer widows". Volunteer fire departments, PTAs, fraternal and charitable organizations from one end of Deer Country to the other throw Opening Day shindigs—Hunters' Breakfasts ("From 3 a.m. to ?") to elaborate game dinners replete with raffles (the usual prize: a deer rifle). "Big Buck" pools abound at gas stations, diners, general stores, VFW Posts, and restaurants throughout Deer Country—put down a buck and you're in; put down a big buck and you win. (The pool at Sherman's General Store in West Rupert, Vermont, where I now hang my hat, amounted to $161 this year. Half of that money went to Mike Jamieson of nearby Arlington, Vermont, who bagged a seven-point, 188-lb. buck; a quarter to the town Parent's Club and the remainder, by draw, to a "Lucky Hunter" whose name was pulled from a hat containing those of all pool entrants. The lucky one proved to be Dude Trueheart, 20, a roly-poly regular on the town road crew. He hardly needed the luck, though, having killed six deer already this season in various eastern states (with both bow and rifle), plus a seven-pointer before Vermont's season opened that he happened to hit on the highway with the town dump truck.

If you doubt that deer season, and especially Opening Day, is a kind of unofficial holiday throughout Deer Country, just try to get hold of a plumber, electrician, or auto mechanic when the magic day rolls around. No amount of whining, cajoling, or even outright bribery will bring him in from deer camp for less than a major emergency. Threats won't work either: remember, he's armed and dangerous. Indeed, a mild kind of madness overcomes the hunter as Opening Day approaches. Most deer seasons in the U.S. are timed to coincide with The Rut (i.e. the mating season for white-tailed deer), which usually occurs in November through most of the animal's range. Many dyed-in-the-Woolrich deer hunters claim, only half joking, that they feel their necks swell as Opening Day nears— "just like a big ol' ten-point buck in The Rut." Unconscious sympathetic magic? You figure it out . . .

In the week or two before Opening Day, symptoms of that madness grow increasing evident. Men who normally rise at a reasonable hour, eat a leisurely breakfast, then zoom off to work at the last minute can be seen betimes, at dawn or dusk, slowly cruising the back roads, their heads swiveling from side to side like F-14 fighter jocks searching for MIGs as they scan the countryside for deer. You're likely to come around a bend in a country road only to find a pickup truck parked in the apex of the corner. As you skid to a halt in a cloud of curses and road dust, the driver will turn from his binoculars and grin, bemused, then point up the hillside. Sure enough a buck . . .

Then there are the pre-season sound effects. Some years I don't know which is louder: the banging of angry hammers as anti-hunters nail up fresh "Posted" signs, or the slow, steady center-fire pop of deer rifles being sighted in. Actually, in my small corner of Deer Country nearly every land owner posts his property lines against trespassers whether he's a Deerslayer or a Bambi Lover. You soon learn who's a serious anti-hunter and who's merely posting his land to keep flatlanders out. On most property, locals are welcome if they'll only muster the courtesy of asking the landowner's permission to hunt. Still, sometimes I feel that Vermont, to be realistic, should change its official state flower from the red clover to the Posted sign.

The ritual of sighting-in has its own minor magic, complete with smells, sounds, and textures that heighten the excitement of the Opening Day to come. There is something sensuous about it all: warm oil on steel and walnut, the banana-peel scent of Hoppe's Nitro Solvent as you push a fresh linen patch through the barrel, the reassuring heft of smooth, bright cartridges as you click them down into the magazine, the rough twist of the leather sling constricting your fore-arm, the greasy snick of the bolt as you seat the first round, the cold curve of the trigger under your forefinger and the first-stage give of the trigger as you tighten up on the sear and the crosshairs split the black bull four ways . . . Then the always-unpredictable slam of the butt-plate into your shoulder when the sear breaks crisply, the explosion of the round unheard (or at least unremarked) but the thwack of the bullet on paper loud and clear. You throw the bolt, the empty brass whirls free, winking at you, and the sharp, rich bite of freshly burned powder blown back on the breeze brings memories of deer seasons past flooding into your mind. Let Proust have his Madeleine; I'll take the smell of a freshly-fired .30-.06 cartridge any day.

There are two ways of sighting in: the confident and the compulsive. Though I'm not one of them anymore, I think the compulsive marksman has more fun. He loads his own brass, fires hundreds of rounds in the course of the year (reaching a ballistic climax in the week before Opening Day) through as many as five or six rifles in as many calibers, and comes away from the exercise with a recoil-bruised shoulder or a fat lip, along with the knowledge that his firearms are now tuned as accurately as possible. Or are they? The doubt always lingers, no matter how many rounds you fire.

The confident marksman, on the other hand, paces off 25 yards from a paper target tacked to a backstop, hunkers down in a sitting position with his elbows braced on his knees, rattles off three rounds, all of which are in the black, and knows in his heart that he'll be on at 200 yards, an inch or so high at 100. The same small fragment of doubt picks away at the back of his mind, but he knows that however many bullets he burns, over whatever ranges with however many rifles, he'll never eradicate it. He's a fatalist. A realist. But the hopeful have more fun . . .

The penultimate rite of preparation for Opening Day is getting your gear together. In the old days, some 40 years ago when I started deer hunting and earlier, you gathered up your red-and-green woolies (lumberjack shirt, hunting coat, Elmer Fudd hat, and your heavy gray Malone or Filson pants), oiled your high-top boots, put an edge on your jackknife, stuck enough bullets to last the season into the loops of our belt, and coiled a length of clothesline with which to drag your buck out of the woods once you'd popped him. If you were a sissy (nowadays you'd call such a hunter a "wuss"), you might bring along a few candy bars to munch if it got too cold on watch, and a compass in case you got lost. Then you grabbed your "crowbar" (as an old mountain-man pal of mine once put it, "A deer rifle's nothin' more than a tool to pry deer out of the hills with") and headed for camp.

Nowadays, thanks in part to such mail order houses as L.L. Bean's, Dunn's, and Cabela's, I'd have to float a second mortgage to afford all the equipment the catalogues tell me I need. I'd have to bathe, shampoo and launder my hunting clothes with Scent Shield soaps (up to $5.95 for an eight-ounce bottle), load up on various costly lotions and potions concocted especially to either lure bucks into range (Robbins' "Censored" Sex Scents include an X-Rated Buck Lure derived from the urine of does in heat at only $19.95 for a four-ounce bottle) or mask my human odor ("Milligan Skunk Essence, Nature's most powerful cover-up . . ." at $3.95 per ounce) and on top of all that, purchase Dick Idol's Whitetail Calling System for $42.95 from Cabela's, consisting of plastic antlers to rattle against one another and imitate the sounds of two bucks fighting over a doe, Dick's "No-Noise" antler carrying kit (you wouldn't want to be walking along through the woods, inadvertently jiggling your antlers, and be jumped from behind by a randy twelve-pointer, would you?), Dick's Enticer Grunt Call, plus an audio cassette to tell you how to make all this stuff work.

For $134.95 I could buy a PortaClimb Climbing Tree Stand and surprise my buck from the sky. For $299 an Electronic Game Counter to monitor deer trails for me in lieu of pre-season scouting ("Each time the infrared beam is broken the counter records the date and time . . . up to 1,000 'events' to accurately record game patterns" up to 30 yards away). And for a mere $139.50, a Two Man Carryall mounted on a bicycle wheel on which to roll—not drag—my buck back to camp. No one has yet offered a robot to stalk, shoot, gralloch, crag, hang, skin, butcher, and cook your deer for you, but it can't be far in the future. A five-figure bargain, I reckon, that will allow you to sit around camp all season, working on your appetite and your whiskey-tan.

The one new technological wrinkle that seems worthwhile is the proliferation of blaze orange hunting garb. Since 1968, when Pennsylvania mandated hunter safety courses and a minimum of 250 sq. in. of blaze orange clothing (about the equivalent of a shooting vest) on every one of the million odd deer hunters who hit Penn's woods each Opening Day, shooting accidents have declined from 560 to 130 a year. "Blaze," as it's commonly called, is highly visible even in the low light of dusk or dawn—the times of day when deer are most often on the move—and can't be mistaken for anything else in nature. The states that now require blaze clothing during hunting seasons report roughly similar results. Vermont remains a holdout, however, and to many Vermonters blaze is anathema.

"They say deer can't see color," allows Clint Perkins, 62, a veteran deer hunter from Rupert, and Dick Raymond's hunting partner for the past 37 years. "But, jeesum, that blaze is so bright that it must stand out from a mile away. It's as bright, even brighter than a deer's white tail, and another deer can sure see that when it's flaggin' away through the woods. One of the scariest things ever happened to me huntin', I was working my way up a mountain one warm day, wearing just a tee-shirt under a green-and-black wool shirt open at the throat on top, and when I got up there I met a guy who'd watched me all the way, 'I had that white vee in my crosshairs the whole way,' he told me, 'I figgered it for that white patch at the base of a deer's throat. Lucky you didn't have horns.'"

But Perkins still hunts in muted colors—blues, reds, or green crosshatched in black—for fear of spooking that big buck of our dreams with the flash of blaze orange. He takes care, though, to wear or carry nothing white. The same applies to most local hunters in Vermont—indeed, one almost certain way to spot a flatlander (i.e. out-of-stater and hence to be held in mild but nonetheless pitiable contempt) is by the amount of blaze he's wearing. Some hunters go all

the way on the visibility/invisibility argument and wear camouflage from top to toe during the rifle season. "I feel safer in camo, with some of these flatlander goons in the woods, than I would in blaze," says one local. "You know the kind I mean—the guys who shoot at anything that moves, then check it later for horns."

Still, this year when I packed my ditty-bag for deer camp, I brought along a blaze orange Jones hat (yea verily, with a magnetic ball compass pinned to its brim—call me wussy, but you can get almighty confused, if not downright lost, when the clouds dip down on these mountains).

Though more and more women are to be seen in the woods of late during deer season (some with chipped fingernails clutching their gunstocks), deer camp as an institution remains pretty much a masculine reserve. Women seem uneasy there, even when they're welcome. Maybe it's all the guns, the mounted deer and bear and bobcat heads gazing down from the pine-paneled walls; maybe it's the raucous card games or the copious flow of stimulants and yarns; maybe it's the mess—in many deer camps I've visited (though not Dick Raymond's), dishes go unwashed for days, dirty boots and clothes litter the environs like the remains of disaster victims, nascent beards proliferate like mung-bean sprouts on gaunt, windburned faces, and the repartee is R-rated at best. No place to take a lady. But guys feel right at home there.

Perhaps William Faulkner caught the primal, masculine allure of the deer camp, or any hunting camp, best in the opening passages of his novella, *The Bear;* ". . . the best game of all, the best of all breathing and forever the best of all listening, the voices quiet and weighty and deliberate for retrospection and recollection and exactitude among the concrete trophies—the racked guns and the heads and skins—in the libraries of town houses or the offices of plantation houses or (and best of all) in the camps themselves where the intact and still-warm meat yet hung, the men who had slain it sitting before the burning logs on hearths, when there were houses and hearths, or about the smoky blazing of piled wood in front of stretched tarpaulins when there were not. There was always a bottle present, so that it would seem . . . that those fine fierce instants of heart and brain and courage and wiliness and speed were concentrated and distilled into that brown liquor which not women, not boys and children, but only hunters drank, drinking not of the blood they spilled but some condensation of the wild immortal spirit, drinking it moderately, humbly even, not with the pagan's base and baseless hope of acquiring thereby the virtues of cunning and strength and speed but in salute to them."

In a good deer camp—and Dick Raymond's is one of the best—the talk is always plain but respectful: of the game and its ways, of the woods and the mountains and the weather, and how things change; of the men who are gone but who hunted these hills and what they saw or did; of the virtues of different weapons or loads under varying conditions; and always of the bucks whose polished antlers (there must be at least five dozen of them accumulated over the 35 years since Raymond founded the camp) rest on a shelf just inside of the door, opposite the stove. Raymond and Clint Perkins can take them down at random, one after the other, and tell you just where and when and with what rifle each was slain, what the weather was doing that day, how the buck reacted to the shot, the precise route by which they dragged it back to camp . . . All of this with loving detail, so well remembered that you know these events—so simplistically dismissed as arrant slaughter compounded with beetle-browed machismo by anti-hunters—amount to little less than sacraments to these men. Every hunter in camp, man, woman or child, is allowed to speak his piece or ask his questions, heard out with a respect too rare in gatherings of Americans nowadays, the insights so gleaned discussed or mildly disputed, the information stowed away in the listeners' minds for future reference.

The food in deer camp is always plain, plentiful, and eminently palatable—perhaps it's the fresh air or the company of boon companions or the eager aura of anticipation that hones the hunter's appetite—and in some camps, downright sumptuous. On the eve of Opening Day in Dick Raymond's camp, eight of us dined on a choice of succulent roast pork or slabs of juicy roast beef, along with potatoes, mashed rutabaga, crisp green beans, slatherings of hellfire horseradish, followed by homebaked apple pie a la mode. Raymond, age 59, is a nationally renowned gardening expert and author of the best-selling *Joy of Gardening*. All the veggies were from his Ferrisburg, Vermont, garden plots, and

they supported his reputation splendidly. But the roasts, over which Dick had lavished special care, were nothing short of superb. "Time enough later in the season for deer liver and onions or spaghetti or leftovers," Raymond said. "But I believe in kicking off Opening Day with a feast. Heck, boys, we've got mountains to climb tomorrow morning!"

Six a.m. of Opening Day—clouds scud low over Bass Hill, scratching their bellies on the spruce tops. I squelch through a boggy meadow toward an alder brake fringing the woods. I've hunted this brake for woodcock and grouse often enough this year to know I might jump deer the moment I enter it, so my rifle—a Remington 700 BDL in 7 mm. Magnum—is at high port, the 3X-9X Variable Bushnell Scope torqued down to three power. "The better to see you with, my deers," I mutter to myself. In close, thick cover like this, you have to get up on your target fast and a scope is sometimes a detriment. Iron sights would be preferable in many Vermont situations—you could see the deer quicker and in depth for a fast shot. But the woods will thin out the higher I work on the mountain, so I chose the scoped rifle over my "brush gun," a .44 Magnum Ruger carbine.

The alders are old—brittle and rotten—and I pick my way carefully so as to snap no branches. The woods are quiet today, sodden from yesterday's rain, but my boots make a sucking noise in the black muck. With a sudden, heart-stopping rattle, a grouse gets up not five yards to my left. I half raise the rifle, startled, then watch it disappear into the ghostly gray gloom. Just as I draw a deep breath to slow my racing pulse, something big erupts from the alders to my right and ahead of me, and goes crashing off uphill—a deer. Its gray-brown shape seems elongated, impossibly buoyant for its bulk and weight as it clears blowdowns and boulders in low, graceful leaps, its long, bushy white tail swaying from side to side like a metronome. The rifle is up, my eye to the scope, but I can't see antlers. Fifty yards out the deer stops, turns sideways, peers back in my direction. Slowly I raise my hand to the scope lever and screw up the power. The deer is standing against a background of bare branches—pale aspens and paper birch—and for a moment I think I see horns. Then the deer shakes its head, lowers it, then raises it again. The putative antlers remain up where they were before she lowered her head. It's a doe, sure enough, but a big one. Try as I might, I can't put horns on her. Now she stamps her forefeet, shakes her pretty head with seeming petulance, and snorts. There's something almost sexy about it, like a beautiful woman angered at some slight.

She stamps and snorts again.

Out of the corner of my eye comes movement. Two more deer, smaller than the big doe, emerge from the alders and pick their way daintily, unconcerned, toward her. I still haven't moved and they don't see me. The wind is from them to me. One is a yearly doe, the second—yes, a baby buck. I can see the gleam of tiny antler buds on his brow. The law in Vermont, as in most states, demands that a deer have at least one antler three inches long before you can drop the hammer on it as a buck. This little fellow might go two inches, maybe two and a half at best. I doubt that he would weigh 80 lbs. dressed out. But even if he were a big spike buck—eight or ten inches on a side and 150 lbs.—I wouldn't shoot him. Not on Opening Day. It just isn't done, or wasn't when I was a youngster anyway. Opening Day is for big bucks. Why fill your tag on the first day of the season with something less than splendid when there's 15 more days to go?

I step forward, snapping branches as I go, and shout, "Hah! Grow up!"

The big doe and her two juvenile offspring spin and bound away, their tails waving back at me in what I think of as The Big White Bye-Bye.

For the next hour or so I still hunt across Bass Hill, taking three or four quiet steps then pausing for an equal length of time, sometimes sitting or standing with my back against a tree but always gazing carefully all around me, alert for the merest flicker of a tail or an ear. Chickadees flirt from branch to branch around me, and at one point when I'm standing still, one makes as if to alight on my gun barrel, but checks off into a shadbush and cocks its head at me. A red squirrel skitters up a tree at my approach and chitters angrily until I pass. I can hear all-terrain-cycles in the distance, chugging and roaring along the old skidder trails that seam these mountains like the crevasses on an old man's face. Damn them! A man should walk, if he's going to kill so fine an animal as a whitetailed buck—pound the hills, work up a sweat, not pollute the wild, quiet woods with snarling pistons and acrid exhaust. Twice in years past, hunters on four-wheelers have spooked deer away from me just as they were getting into range. One of them was at least a six-point buck. There oughta be a law . . .

By 9 a.m. I'm up in The Oven—a great gouge in the western flank of Bear Mountain down which run many spring-fed rills and two waterfalls which, when the temperature and humidity conditions are just right, produce great boiling clouds of mist, thus giving The Oven its name. There are many old cellar holes up here, memorials to long-dead generations of Vermonters who farmed this hardscrabbled hollow. It must have been a rough life: a few chickens, maybe a cow or two, a herd of Merino sheep grazing on the meadows below, an orchard of hardy apples (whose progeny even today feed grouse and deer and bears each fall) and a small garden patch dominated by root crops. Wild meat was important to survival in those days before game laws and even now—old traditions dying hard—I'm sometimes awakened at night (winter of summer) by the hollow center-fire pop of a jacklighter's rifle. I don't begrudge them their meat. Rural poverty is endemic, ineradicable in backwoods New England . . .

A fusillade of shots half a mile away snaps me out of my reverie. I can distinguish at least four of five different calibers of rifle among it. Probably those damn flatlanders who've taken to parking up near the Snow Place, got a deer running amongst them and everyone taking a poke at it. There's an old saying in Wisconsin, where I grew up, usually attributed to a wise old Indian: "One shot, buck. Two shots, maybe buck. Three shots, no buck." I can only hope that they've missed. One thing about Opening Day, you take your chances as the Good Lord provides. With hundreds of hunters poking around anywhere within earshot, deer tend to panic. Creatures of habit normally, they're likely to appear anywhere on Opening Day once the boots begin to trample and the rifle start to speak. I watch the woods intently in the direction from which the fusillade came. Sure enough, in a few minutes I see movement—gray-brown fourlegged forms sifting down through the brush toward Oven Brook. One, two—yes, three of them. A quarter of a mile away still, if they're an inch. I scan them through my scope. Four years ago in a similar situation I had the privilege of watching the biggest white-tail buck of my life emerge into my sights. That was up on top of The Oven. Up among the wind-warped, stunted spruces and dwarf beech on the crest. He had been chased up there by hunters down below, and for just a brief moment as he scrambled over the ledges and stopped to look back, I could have taken him. He was probably 500 yards away, but with this rifle I've killed antelope—both African and pronghorn—at that range. This buck was gunmetal blue against the snow, with dark beams and brilliant white tines on his rack, tall tines, at least four of them on a side. With his brow points he would have been a ten-pointer. Maybe more. He looked thick and long to me, with wide square shoulders and a swollen neck, and he tossed his head impatiently as he paused there on the ledge, plumes of frosty steam blowing from his ten-gauge nostrils. I held on the line of his backbone with the vertical crosshair bobbing lightly to my heartbeat just behind his shoulder and took up the tension in the trigger . . .

But I couldn't break the shot. I still don't know why. Or maybe I do. Five hundred yards was just too far. What if I missed his heart/lung area? What if I gut shot him—that sodden thunk, white hair flying, and when you get over to where he'd stood as you shot you found dark blood with gray-green swatches of half digested vegetable matter? What if you were sure of him and the bullet hit a twig enroute and deflected to the left just far enough to plunk in his paunch? How would you feel then, Mister Sureshot, with a long, sad trudge ahead of you down his rapidly cooling blood trail, seeing where he'd lain up and the blood (now black) had pooled and frozen on the bitter leaves, then got up with his back hunched at the pain in his belly and walked on, stronger now with the wound not bleeding (but death in him as certainly as you pulled the trigger) to disappear somewhere on the slopes of Mother Myrick Mountain, food tomorrow for the coydogs and ravens?

So I didn't shoot that buck. But half an hour later some hunter from New Jersey did. Just over the ridge from The Oven. It had to be him. The buck dressed out at 221 lbs. and wore twelve points on his antlers.

But now it's Opening Day again and three deer are walking into range. I watch them closely as they emerge from the brush and pick their way across Oven Brook. The first one's a doe—a big one. The second one is also hornless.

Could be a buck trailing after them, letting them cross first to draw fire. Could be a buck—and it is. That same little rascal I'd seen earlier this morning—that 80 lb. pencil-point from out of the alder brake. I put down the rifle and laugh. It's the same trio of deer I'd jumped four hours ago, still meandering across the face of The Oven and back, meaty slow-motion shuttlecocks bunted back and forth across the face of the mountain by hunting pressure. That's modern-day deer hunting for you.

As I start down the mountain for camp, I can hear the road hunters moving along the rutted dirt roads in the hollows. It's always this way—come mid-morning of Opening Day, hunters emerge from the woods where they've been since dawn, sitting or still-hunting or perhaps participating on a drive (a cooperative effort in which one group of hunters progressively "beats" a piece of terrain in hopes of driving deer to another group on the "watch line" waiting with ready rifles). Then they all get in their cars or trucks and drive the roads, hoping to spot moving deer along the way. In most states, game laws forbid shooting from a motor vehicle or a right-of-way, but road hunters pay no attention to the niceties. If a buck is spotted, they just lean out the window (or at best over the hood) and cut loose. Damn them, as well as the four-wheelers. All day long through the deer season, trucks and cars—some of them swank BMWs or Lincolns or Cadillacs—prowl the road in front of my house, their windows full of squinty eyes.

As I hiked along toward camp, the tune of Eppridge's predawn ditty came back to me, marking time to my footsteps. I thought of what we would do with the rest of Opening Day, which already felt about a week long. Bill had spent the morning making pictures of hunters checking in their deer at Sherman's General Store in West Rupert. Dick Raymond was hunting the ridge across the hollow from Haystack but would be back to camp for lunch with an after-action report (if he hadn't connected with the buck of his dreams and been forced to spend the rest of the day dragging it out). Clint Perkins was hunting on nearby Masters Mountain with his 11-year-old grandson, Josh Sprague, a blond, bespectacled, quiet young kid still a year away from the legal age for deer hunting in Vermont but just the right age for Perk to inculcate him with the traditions of fair-chase. Josh wouldn't carry a rifle this year but he'd sure carry a lot of woods-lore by the time the day had ended. During the course of the afternoon, other hunters would drop by camp to swap Opening Day experiences, most of them empty-handed but a few with bucks in the beds of their pickups or peering glaze-eyed out of the trunks of their cars. Toward dusk we'd all head out again, into the woods, to hunt until dark or cold or frustration, rarely success, drove us back to camp. Some would head for the Game Supper in nearby Pawlet, Vermont, where they would dine heartily on the meat of road-killed or donated deer, bear, raccoon and partridge, along with cole slaw, beans, potatoes, and an enticing array of homebaked pies—all for only $_____ a

serving. Others would kick back in camp, pour themselves a drink, and shoot the bull (not the buck) until it was time for supper and another game of poker. Opening Day would be behind them, the rest of the season to come.

As I neared the road, the sound of blatting engines grew louder. Eppridge's tune still marked time in my head, but now I had words of my own for it:

The trucks come grumbling down the road
All of them in low gear.
They're loaded with guys with blood in their eyes,
All of them searching for deer.
"A buck!" comes the shout and the rifles poke out
"Blam! Blam!"—how the bullets fly.
Bambi the Buck is flat outta luck,
And today is a good day to die.
He'll bound, he'll bound, he'll leap all around,
He'll run until he's finally downed:
Today's the day of the road-hunters' killing orgy . . .

Yes—damn the road hunters, and the four-wheelers, the slob-hunters hung with their Bowie knives and walkie-talkies and electronic "Bionic Ears," their high-tech shortcuts to what the game managers call "hunter success". Rambos in blaze-orange drag. But God bless the running deer, and the few men and women and children who still hunt them the old way—on foot, with respect, quietly. They are the last of the real hunters. And God bless their Opening Day.

My comment to the animal rights leaders is that if I could agree with their views, life would be much simpler for me, whereas if they agreed with me, they would be unemployed.

—WALTER E. HOWARD

WE DAKOTANS REJECT ANIMAL ACTIVISTS.
FURS, GAME, FISH & LIVESTOCK
ARE OUR ECONOMY

In the woods we return to reason and faith.

—RALPH WALDO EMERSON

Hunters are often dreamers, fixing their gaze on some mythical and faraway paradise where bucks bed behind every bush and wear racks like a wad of barbed wire.

—NORM STRUNG

In hunting, the finding and killing of the game is after all but a part of the whole. The free, self-reliant, adventurous life, with its rugged and stalwart democracy; the wild surroundings, the grand beauty of the scenery, the chance to study the ways and habits of the woodland creatures—all these unite to give to the career of the wilderness hunter its peculiar charm.

—THEODORE ROOSEVELT

The first track is the end of a string. At the far end, a being is moving; a mystery, dropping a hint about itself every so many feet, telling you more about itself until you can almost see it, even before you come to it.

—TOM BROWN

... We found the antelope extremely shy and watchful insomuch that we had been unable to get a shot at them. When at rest they generally select the most elevated point in the neighborhood. They are watchful and extremely quick of sight and their sense of smelling very acute it is almost impossible to approach them within gunshot. In short, they will frequently discover and flee from you at the distance of three miles.

—MERIWETHER LEWIS, SEPT. 17, 1804

The most beguiling moment in the hunt is the first moment of the encounter.

—BARRY LOPEZ

The power contained in huge racks is so great that it can stir the ardor . . . in even the most pragmatic of subsistence hunters . . .

—THOMAS MCINTYRE

To brag a little, to lose well, to crow gently if in luck . . . to pay up, to own up, to shut up . . . are the virtues of a good sportsman.

—OLIVER WENDELL HOLMES

When one thinks of the enormous strength of the 'silver,' which can overpower the mightiest steer, and bend and break its neck or tear its shoulder from its body at a stroke, one is able to say, 'Do not hunt a bear unless thy skin is not dear to thee.'

—Frederic Remington, circa 1895

Killing has a place in hunting . . . I see it as a rite, a sacrifice, an acknowledgement of the sport's origin . . . But never as an end in itself.

—RODERICK HAIG-BROWN

...The best part of hunting and fishing was the thinking about going and the talking about it after you got back.

—ROBERT RUARK

. . . Deep in the guts of most men is buried the involuntary response to the hunter's horn, a prickle of the nape hairs, an acceleration of the pulse, an atavistic memory of his fathers, who killed first with stone, and then with club, and then with spear, and then with bow, and then with gun, and finally with formulae . . . somewhere in the pigeon chest of the clerk is still the vestigial remnant of the hunter's heart; somewhere in his nostrils the half-forgotten smell of blood.

—ROBERT RUARK

I thought I had climbed to the moon the first time I ventured into wild sheep territory. Then I went on my first goat hunt. You'll know you're in goat country when it takes both arms and both legs to climb and you can spit down on sheep.

—PATRICK STEPHENS

The hunter is the arch-type of freedom. His well-being rests in no man's hands save his own.

—THEODORE ROOSEVELT

For me the complexion of a hunt changes when meat is in camp. I get edgy and sleep fitfully. I know that a veritable highway of scent is drifting over the forest and tundra, a lure few bears can resist.

—Tom Walker

There is a pioneer spirit that follows the hunter who travels by canoe. There is magic and drama to floating a river, for you get a front row seat in the theatre of streamside ecology. Each bend is both a quest and a question, and rivers are, ultimately, metaphors on the hunter's life.

—JOHNATHON L. MORGAN

. . . It is characteristic of hunting to have hardly changed in its general structure since ancient times. The marvelous scene of a deer hunt in the Cueva de los Caballos [Cave of Horses] in the Castellon province of Valencia, which dates from the Paleolithic Age, does not differ in any important way from a photograph of a [modern] hunting party.

—JOSE ORTEGA Y GASSET

Fall belongs to the hunter, if for no other reason than winter demands it.

—Guy De La Valdene

*A peculiar virtue in wildlife ethics is that the
hunter ordinarily has no gallery to applaud or
disapprove of his conduct. Whatever his acts, they
are dictated by his own conscience, rather than by
a mob of onlookers. It is difficult to exaggerate the
importance of this fact. Voluntary adherence to an
ethical code elevates the self-respect of the sportsman,
but it should not be forgotten that voluntary dis-
regard of the code degenerates and depraves him.*

—ALDO LEOPOLD

The chances of your hitting a two-inch sapling at
100 yards are directly proportional to the size of
the buck standing behind it.

—AARON FRASER PASS

There are only two who should never be questioned: God and the camp cook, for both hold your fate in their hands.

—MICHAEL McGURTY, "DINING OUT"

At the center of any great hunt is the campfire. You can dry your boots by it, warm your toes over it, and tell lies around it.

—GERALD CUMMINGS

The tundra shrubs were ablaze in the red and gold of late autumn, and the great vault of Arctic sky domed it all. Here a man is just another player on a vast and ancient stage and not nearly so omnipotent as elsewhere he might imagine himself to be.

—AARON FRASER PASS

Hunting in my experience . . . is a state of mind. All of one's faculties are brought to bear in an effort to become fully incorporated into the landscape.

—BARRY LOPEZ

THE FOURTH DAY

By Lionel Atwill

After two scotches and a lunch of yellow potato salad, a flaccid pickle, ham and cheese hidden in a hard roll, and an indecipherable sweet wrapped so securely in foil that one might imagine it glutinous filling containing nuclear waste, I found what might make life complete: a Desk Director System 600, only $995.00. Technology, I thought, is the god of contemporary man.

I found the Director in a Sharper Image catalogue hidden in the seat pocket behind the barf bag. "A quantum leap in desktop efficiency," according to the copy, the Director was eight square feet of greasy black leather wed to a phone, a "vacuum fluorescent" display panel, and more buttons than I have fingers. It did everything: compute, place calls, store numbers, flash the date and time.

And there was so much more? The Wizard of Wine, a digital sommelier in burgundy plastic that winked its LCDs appreciatively at a '49 Mouton-Rothschild. An electronic ocean (with rain and waterfall features) to soothe the harried with the gentle rhythm of crashing water. A pith helmet sporting a solar-powered fan.

Had the plane not landed at Denver, and had I not had to sprint for my connection to Steamboat Springs, I would have ordered them all. Life could be so pleasant, lubricated by technology, organized by quantum leaps of desktop efficiency.

But for now, they would have to wait. More intrinsic things took precedence: elk.

My friends Bob and Bart and I were bound for the mountains. For the black timber. For a week we had contemplated for a year. For a chance to call in and bow-hunt rutting bulls.

We had arranged with an outfitter to hunt his leased ten thousand acres and to stay at his tent camp and eat his wife's food. But we had insisted that the hunting would be according to our plans. At our pace. We wanted to do this one ourselves: find the elk, call in a bull, drop him with an arrow, and get him out.

We took an open jeep to camp over a webwork of dirt roads that twisted through farms and around mountains. We traveled silently, sucking in dust with each breath, until the road narrowed to parallel ruts and the guide said, "This is it." The trip had taken an hour, and when we pulled up next to the tent, another ten minutes passed while we cleared our lungs and wiped off our glasses, drained our bladders, and unloaded our gear.

And then we could take it all in: the mountain rising above us, a rupture in the plains, dark with spruce, dark and foreboding; the small grove of aspen behind the tent with three horses and a mule standing in its shade; the cook tent, its doorway framing the guide's wife wiry and smiling, a pot of hot coffee in her outstretched hand; and a game rack inordinately high to my eye, until it hit me that elk are four times the size of deer. "Great, beautiful," we muttered, because that was all we could think to say, and we disappeared into our tent to shuck our traveling clothes and put on hunting gear.

The elk, we were told by the guide, lay in the black timber, shaded from the heat of the day. We would have to climb, starting early so we could approach them upwind, from the top of the mountain down. And we did.

We got up at three, something none of us would do for any reason but to hunt. We drank lots of coffee and held silent conversations of nods and looks. Then the time came to put aside the dreams and the talk and really do it, do what we had thought about for the year, so we climbed the mountain.

We were enthusiastic but awkward that first day, our bodies out of sync with the rough country—panting, slipping, sliding, falling, making too much noise, seeing too little sign, sweating in the heat of midday. We would stop and call, "Ough-weeeeeee-ugh, yugh, yugh, yugh," but without great conviction, not knowing if we sounded like elk or merely like fools. Our momentum came from memories of meetings and phone calls and plans and practice back home, not from any inner drive, not from a hunter's soul. Not yet, at least. But we did it all the same.

That evening we held to the ritual—drinking straight from a bottle, smoking evil black cigars, and telling exaggerated tales of the day. Our good humor came less from satisfaction with our hunt than from a need to hold to the script we had written. Soon, though the reality of the day surpassed the fantasy of our drama. Tired, dehydrated, frustrated to a degree, we went to bed.

On the second day we drank twice as much coffee. Bart limped noticeably, bruised from a fall. The bravado was gone; we had had one chance and had not found our game. Now we knew we would have to sweat and suffer, to battle not only the cunning of the animal but the heat, the blowdown, the brush, the rocks, the branches that slap faces and trip feet, and our own growing reluctance to pain, to keep to our plan. (Where did it come from? we began to wonder. Whoever thought we could hunt this creature? Whoever thought we would want to?)

We were late getting started that second day. Gray morning light was chasing shadows from the trees where we left the cook tent. The elk, we knew, would now be making their daily pilgrimage from lowland feed to the black timber. We had missed those subtle predawn minutes when the forest guard changes, when the night feeders turn to twittering birds. We cherished those last minutes by the camp stove, coffee in hand, more than the primordial lure of the mountain. Yet we felt guilt in missing the first hour of hunting light.

By accident, perhaps by intention, we met up in the woods toward noon and frittered away several hours over talk and food and tobacco. We had seen sign, all of us, but no elk as yet. Might as well enjoy ourselves, we thought, and we stretched out for an hour nap before separating again to work slowly down the mountain to camp.

But things changed that evening. Bart had seen a bull. Not across a high park or on a far ridge, but up close, where the musty smell of the beast drifted to him, where he could watch muscle ripple beneath coarse hide, where he could hear branches crack under hooves and limbs brush against polished antlers. Very close, but not close enough for a shot. Yet the presence of that beast steeled Bart, renewed his vigor. He drank hard from his bottle of rum and smiled and laughed. His purpose had returned. He was anxious for the morning. His enthusiasm fueled Bob and me, but at the same time we were jealous of his small triumph.

On the third day we knew where the elk lay. We reached the woods well before dawn, split up, as was our custom, and climbed. As the sun came up, our calls cried from three ridges. Nothing answered. We pushed the mountain hard now, and our bodies cooperated. The stumbling was over. Eyes and ears were attuned to the woods, but some element was still missing: a sense of the animal. We knew, intellectually, where he fed, where he slept, where he rolled in piss-dampened mud, but intellect fell shy of telling us when.

But we were close. A cow and calf moved past Bob in the late afternoon, out of sight but near enough for him to hear the young elk's weak blats. Bob had tracked them, following prints and droppings through the black timber. They never knew he was there.

Bart returned to the place where he had seen a bull and in the distance spotted a spike moving up a trail. He called, but his squeals and grunts intimidated the young animal. It answered once, and desertion, then trotted off.

I saw no elk but I came on fresh tracks and glistening dung, which I picked up without hesitation to feel its warmth and to know then, that I was close to the animal, close in distance, closer in mind.

That night we didn't talk much. We discussed what we would do in the morning, but it was perfunctory conversation; we knew now where each of us chose to hunt. We ate our food with purpose and drank some whiskey before going to our tent. We had washed our clothes that afternoon, and now in the flickering yellow light of a lantern, we collected them from a makeshift line and stored them outside in plastic bags with small twigs of spruce. We touched up our arrows, laid out clean socks, and went to bed.

The clock didn't have a chance to ring in the morning. We woke, dressed quickly, and got to the cook tent before the coffee boiled. Bart put on camouflage while he ate his eggs, and Bob, usually chatty in the morning, merely mumbled through a mouthful of toast and potatoes as he pored over a topographical map.

I felt wide awake long before I should have, full of energy light-footed and sharp-eyed. It was a feeling I've known in athletics; confidence that comes after much practice, a sense of being able to do almost anything well and without thought. We all had it; even the guide, who had spent most of his days sprawled in a hammock at camp, was wired.

By jeep we drove halfway up the mountain, then checked our gear, slung quivers and daypacks, pissed, waved, and started to climb. The sun had yet to show itself, but the first birds of morning were tuning, and a rustle in the bushes told us deer were returning from their nightlong feed.

I reached the summit in darkness and, damp form the sweat of my climb, shucked my shirt and pulled on a sweater I carried in my pack, then sat on a rock to watch the sunrise. The cold, damp morning air, which normally I escaped in folds of wool, today felt invigorating. I could taste the oxygen in it, and the scents it brought me—damp earth, spruce, a skunk in the distance—were true and sweet. The birds were louder now and the black sky began to fade to light. And in the distance an elk called.

I find great pleasure in moving well through the woods. There is poetry in a patient stalk—one step, a breath, a hard look to cut through the gloom and the trees, to pick out a creature before it picks out you. This day I stalked well. I worked along the barren ridge of the mountain, just beneath the crest so as not to be caught in silhouette on top. As I came on an outcrop that would force me from my path, I stopped and heard on the far side the rhythm of something walking. I drew an arrow, nocked it and dropped slowly to a crouch.

Above the rock appeared a mule deer, first antlers, then head, eyes, neck, body, and legs. He moved casually like a kid coming home from school, a foot-dragging, offhand gait. He was a big deer, the best I had seen. I watched as he moved toward me, then drew. I laid the arrow on his chest. It was an easy shot, fifteen yards, quartering toward me. But I let off. The lure of the elk was too strong now, and should I shoot this deer, I would spend the day and part of the night dragging him down the mountain. There was time in the evening for mule deer, down on the flats where a jeep could do the work. He dropped down the mountain on the far side. He never knew I there; I felt good about that.

Below the ridge lay the black timber, dense spruce clogged with blowdowns where the elk liked to bed. I headed there to call. In the woods I found piles of droppings and trails freshly scarred from elk's hooves. They had been here yesterday, I now knew; they would be here today, I thought. I found a big blowdown and put my back to it, nocked an arrow, and called. No answer, so I waited ten minutes and called again. Still no elk. The bull I had heard at first light had moved to a draw to the east, I thought, but another

should come here, so I called again and again, five or six times over the hour.

No elk answered, none appeared. I decided to move down the hill toward the lower ridge where Bob had seen the cow and calf. Staying in the shadows, I walked at the pace of an old man through the trees. I took four hours to get down the mountain. Twice I jumped deer from the cover of a streambed; the second stood and watched me from thirty feet, and I knew that I was moving well, so well that the deer did not know exactly what I was. I could have shot the second, like the big buck on top, but I didn't. Elk on the mind.

But not on the mountain. In midafternoon I broke into the sagebrush. Bob stood by some rutted jeep tracks leading back to camp; he too had seen no elk. But neither of us was disappointed. We both felt keyed to the woods, to the animals, to what was now a mission. We decided to go back to camp and rest for a few hours, then return to two water holes by which we both had passed. Deer tracks skewered the ground around the water, and we reasoned that the deer would move there toward evening to drink. An elk might not go down this day, but surely something else would.

We should have been able to sleep, but we couldn't, couldn't even stand to stay in camp more than an hour. The mountain was our siren now, and the louder she called, the harder we drove ourselves. Bob and I hiked back to the water holes by way of another ridge. We hunted along the way. Bob did the calling; I scouted for fresh sign. We picked up a well-used deer trail leading to the water holes, and by the time we got to them, we were pretty sure we would get a buck tonight.

Bob dropped off at the first hole. I walked three hundred yards to the second and found some good cover in a clump of stubby evergreens. I cut shooting lanes, got comfortable, and settled in.

I've been bored waiting for my wife, waiting for trains and planes, waiting for half-time to end in the Super Bowl, but I've never been bored waiting for game. When the stand is good and you have camouflaged yourself well, when you know you can shoot over 270 degrees, when the wind goes down and the shadows stretch out under the honey light of evening, there is too much to do to get bored. Just listening carries such intensity that a mouse scrambling through the duff is louder than a rush-hour freeway; a deer foot falling is a kettledrum's beat. Smells and sights are amplified beyond reason, and time's passage is condensed.

So it was in my clump. An hour passed, an hour and a half. The time of half-light came when animals move and visibility fades. I rocked forward on my haunches like the predator I was and tensed. Then, high on the mountain, came the trilling call of an elk.

Great confrontations are charted in advance, I believe, and this one had been written over the year, perhaps over the centuries. But it was not to be mine. I had forgotten to bring my call; Bob had his. He answered the bull, the animal replied, and I knew that I would be but a spectator to this hunt. Because I was so close, however, close in distance, and close in a bond that had formed with Bob over twelve months of preparation and over four days on the mountain, close to an animal that now possessed me, there was no jealousy. As the bull bellowed again, then tore up a small tree not a hundred yards from me, jealousy would have been too refined an emotion to consider, for my every instinct was focused on the elk. I was a predator, part of the pack.

The elk came in. I heard him attack another tree, then call again. Bob replied softly; he was the challenging bull, unsure of his rival, perhaps intimidated. The elk charged through the brush. A hush enveloped the mountain.

I waited twenty minutes in my clump of trees. No rational thought compelled me to stay there, no ponderous analysis: "If A equals B, then I should do C." My guts told me to sit tight; my guts told me to watch for that bull, to deep my arrow ready. And then they told me to move. Stealthily, I crawled out of the spruce. I skirted Bob's position and dropped into the grass near his water hole.

Then from the tree line a hundred yards away I heard the elk's death rattle—a mournful bellow, the sound of life escaping, played to the throb of my own beating heart. And silence.

We met beside the water hole, waited in silence for half an hour, then tracked him down. Bob's arrow had taken him above the heart, piercing lungs and liver, draining him of blood in less than a quarter-hour. God, he was big: five points to a side, the tines still coated with fresh mud and strips of the trees he had thrashed. We could barely turn him over to make the first cut, and after gutting him, we had trouble dragging him three feet to slant his body so the blood would drain. By the light of a flashlight, we dressed him out. My hands trembled; I felt a reverence for this beast. His quartering was a sacred rite. Later, back at camp, at night when the meat was hung and the hide salted, the head caped and ivory pulled and polished, we fried up great ropes of tenderloins, rare and tender, and reverently ate them: our communion of the fourth day.

We hunted on for two days more, but our appetites for the kill were blunted. We worked, but not with the drive that came from the pits of our stomachs on that fourth day. Some primordial notion told us that the meat was in, that eight hundred pounds of elk is enough for three men. I ambushed a cow on a trail and drew on her at ten yards, but didn't fire. Bart had shot at a spike bull and passed too. We were not being sentimental; we just didn't feel the need. The rite had been celebrated. We had transcended the need to prove ourselves, to put antlers on the wall. Our motivation to hunt and kill that mighty beast had come from a more atavistic source, which had possessed us on that fourth day.

Then it was over. We fortified with whiskey to face the world and to drive off the remorse that came when we left the black timber for the blacktop of town. And how quickly the transition was made. In hours we were in an airport, in the cramped seats of a plane, and then, with my mind still on a mountain, I flipping through a catalogue—a bible preaching blissful existence through technology. I wondered if someday, a million generations from now, men would be possessed by an atavistic yearning for digital convenience, for flashing lights and electronic waves. Somehow, I thought, it would never measure up. Some things we can live without.

. . . The wild ram embodies the mystery and the magic of the mountains, the rocky canyons, the snowy peaks, the fragrant alpine meadows, the gray slide rock, the icy, dancing rills fed by snowbank and glacier, the sweet clean air of the high places, and the sense of being alone on the top of the world with the eagles, the marmots, and the wild sheep themselves.

—JACK O'CONNOR

For the first-time visitor into bear country, there is—or should be—a sober understanding that there is another predator in the area that cannot be counted on to run at the sight of man.

—SETH THORSEN

...In the coldest midwinter weather, not a breath of wind may stir; and then the still, merciless, terrible cold that broods over the earth like the shadow of silent death seems even more dreadful in its gloomy rigor than is the lawless madness of the storms.

—THEODORE ROOSEVELT

For the caribou hunter, life is planned around weather systems, which is to say day-to-day. There are no weather reports on the Barren Ground and to look skyward is to know as much as any man what the weather might hold.

—SETH THORSEN

The ups and downs of sheep hunting contain a disproportionate number of 'ups.' It's all leg and lung and mostly leg. Long hikes, tricky river crossings, and hard climbs on steep slopes of loose scree while wearing a 40-pound pack and sometimes wearing hip boots, are the price of admission to sheep country.

—Aaron Fraser Pass

To him who has scented the trackless wilds, and whose blood has gone the pace of its perils and freedom, there comes, every now and again, an irresistible impulse to fly from electric lights, railroads, and directories; to travel on his feet instead of being jerked along in a cable-car; to find his way with the aid of a compass and the North Star, instead of by belettered lamp-posts.

—CASPAR WHITNEY, CIRCA 1895

From that day on I have been a lover of mule deer . . . They were my first love and still remain my strongest . . . somehow the sight of an old mule deer buck, head high, antlers lying along his broad back, returns me definitely to my childhood and the day I first felt the mystery of wild game and wild country.

—JACK O'CONNOR

May the gods grant us all space to carry a sturdy bow and wander through the forest glades to seek the bounding deer; to lie in the deep meadow grasses; to watch the flight of birds; to smell the fragrance of burning leaves; to cast an upward glance at the unobserved beauty of the moon. May they give us strength to draw the string to the cheek, the arrow to the barb and loose the flying shaft, so long as life may last.

—Saxton Pope

He is the oddest assortment of parts—goggle eyes, barrel chest, and legs like lathe-turned dowels . . .
—THOMAS MCINTYRE

There was a Russian school of acting which once maintained stoutly that a good tragic actor had to suffer. The same must be true of all hunters... The value of a trophy is computed directly in terms of personal investment in its acquisition.

—ROBERT RUARK

Forestry may prescribe for a certain area either a mixed stand or a pure one. But game management should always prescribe a mixed stand—that is, the perpetuation of every indigenous species.

—ALDO LEOPOLD

I see no reason to apologize for being a hunter, particularly in this age. What comparable sweetness, mystery, and wonder can be found in the Styrofoam-dished, Saran-wrapped, boneless, skinless chicken breasts at the meat counter of the supermarket?

—JIM FERGUS

From the white-knuckled passenger's point of view, a bush plane landing on tundra or a gravel bar is pretty much a controlled crash.

—AARON FRASER PASS

Among all the animals with which they are familiar, there is none more impressive to the minds of the Eastern Cree than the black bear. Its courage, sagacity, and above all, its habit of walking manlike, upon its hind legs, have convinced the Indians of its supernatural propensities.

—ALONSON SKINNER

...The gathering, cooking, and eating of wild game as part of your daily diet in camp is as much a part of big game hunting as the snicker of a horse or the whisper of snow upon a canvas roof.

—NORM AND SIL STRUNG

*I grew up dreaming of the boreal forest with giant
moose stalking the timber. Years later, when a
home in the bush was a reality, a moose passing the
cabin brought a special satisfaction. I'd escaped.
I lived a childhood dream. And it was good.*

—Tom Walker

THE HEART OF THE GAME

By T. McGuane

Hunting in your own back yard becomes with time, if you love hunting, less and less expeditionary. This year, when Montana's eager frosts knocked my garden on its butt, the hoe seemed more like the rifle than it ever had before, the vegetables more like game.

My son and I went scouting before the season and saw some antelope in the high plains foothills of the Absaroka Range, wary, hanging on the skyline; a few bands and no great heads. We crept around, looking into basins, and at dusk met a tired cowboy on a tired horse followed by a tired blue-heeler dog. The plains seemed bigger than anything, bigger than the mountains that seemed to sit in the middle of them, bigger than the ocean. The clouds made huge shadows that traveled on the grass slowly through the day.

Hunting season trickles on forever, if you don't go in on a cow with anybody. There is the dark argument of the empty deep-freeze against headhunting ("You can't eat horns!"). But nevertheless, in my mind, I've laid out the months like playing cards, knowing some decent whitetails

127

could be down in the river bottom and, fairly reliably, the long windy shots at antelope. The big buck mule deer—the ridge runners—stay up in the scree and rock walls until the snow drives them out; but they stay high long after the elk have quit and broken down the hay corrals on the ranches and farmsteads, which, when you're hunting the rocks from a saddle horse, look pathetic and housebroken with their yellow lights against the coming of winter.

Where I live, the Yellowstone River runs straight north, then takes an eastward turn at Livingston, Montana. This flowing north is supposed to be remarkable; and the river doesn't do it long. It runs mostly over sand and stones once it comes out of the rock slots near the Wyoming line. But all along, there are deviations of one sort or another: canals, backwaters, sloughs; the red willows grow in the sometimes flooded bottom, and at the first elevation, the cottonwoods. I hunt here for the white-tailed deer which in recent years have moved up these rivers in numbers never seen before.

The first morning, the sun came up hitting around me in arbitrary panels as the light moved through the jagged openings in the Absaroka Range. I was walking very slowly in the edge of the trees, the river invisible a few hundred yards to my right, but sending a huge sigh through the willows. It was cold and the sloughs had crowns of ice thick enough to support me. As I crossed one great clear pane, trout raced around under my feet and a ten-foot bubble advanced slowly before my cautious steps. Then passing back into the trees, I found an active game trail, cut cross-lots to pick a better

stand, sat in a good vantage place under a cottonwood with the aught-six across my knees. I thought, running my hands up into my sleeves: This is lovely, but I'd rather be up in the hills; and I fell asleep.

I woke up a couple hours later, the coffee and early morning drill having done not one thing for my alertness. I had drooled on my rifle and it was time for my chores back at the ranch. My chores of late had consisted primarily of working on screenplays so that the bank didn't take the ranch. These days the primary ranch skill is making the payment; it comes before irrigation, feeding out, and calving. Some rancher friends find this so discouraging they get up and roll a number or have a slash of tanglefoot before they even think of the glories of the West. This is the New Rugged.

The next day, I reflected upon my lackadaisical hunting and left really too early in the morning. I drove around to Mission Creek in the dark and ended up sitting in the truck up some wash listening to a New Mexico radio station until my patience gave out and I started out cross-country in the dark just able to make out the nose of the Absaroka Range as it faced across the river to the Crazy Mountains. I went maddeningly up and down slick banks and a couple of times I had game clatter out in front of me in the dark. Then I turned up a long coulee that climbed endlessly south, and started in that direction, knowing the plateau on top should hold some antelope. After half an hour or so, I heard the mad laughing of coyotes, throwing their voices all around the inside of the coulee trying to panic rabbits, and making my hair stand on end despite my affection for them. The stars tracked overhead into the first pale light, and it was nearly dawn before I came up on the bench. I could hear cattle below me and I moved along an edge of thorn trees to break my outline, then sat down at the point to wait for shooting light.

I could see antelope on the skyline before I had that light; and by the time I did, there was a good big buck angling across from me, looking at everything. I thought I could see well enough, and I got up into a sitting position and into the sling. I had made my moves quietly, but when I looked through the scope the antelope was two hundred yards out, using up the country in bounds. I tracked with him, let him bounce up into the eticle, and touched off a shot. He was down and still, but I sat watching until I was sure.

Nobody who loves to hunt feels absolutely hunky-dory when the quarry goes down. The remorse spins out almost before anything and the balancing act ends on one declination or another. I decided that unless I become a vegetarian, I'll get my meat by hunting for it. I feel absolutely unabashed by the arguments of other carnivores who get their meat in plastic with blue numbers on it. I've seen slaughterhouses, and anyway, as Sitting Bull said, when the buffalo are gone, we will hunt mice, for we are hunters and we want our freedom.

The antelope had piled up in the sage, dead before he hit the ground. He was an old enough buck that the tips of his pronged horns were angled in toward each other. I turned him downhill to bleed him out. The bullet had mushroomed in the front of the lungs, so the job was already halfway done. With antelope, proper field dressing is critical because they can end up sour if they've been run or haphazardly hogdressed. And they sour from their own body heat more than from external heat.

The sun was up and the big buteo hawks were lifting on the thermals. There was enough breeze that the grass began to have directional grain like the prairie, and the rim of the coulee wound up away from me toward the Absaroka. I felt peculiarly solitary, sitting on my heels next to the carcass in the sagebrush and greasewood, my rifle racked open on the ground. I made an incision around the metatarsal glands inside the back legs and carefully removed them and set them well aside; then I cleaned the blade of my hunting knife with handfuls of grass to keep from tainting the meat with those powerful glands. Next I detached the anus and testes from the outer walls and made a shallow puncture below the sternum, spread it with the thumb and forefinger of my left hand and ran the knife upside down to the bone bridge between the hind legs. Inside, the diaphragm was like the taut lid of a drum and cut away cleanly, so that I could reach clear up to the back of the mouth and detach the windpipe. Once that was done I could draw the whole visceral package out onto the grass and separate out the heart, liver, and tongue before propping the carcass open with two whittled-up sage scantlings.

You could tell how cold the morning was despite the exertion, just by watching the steam roar from the abdominal cavity. I stuck the knife in the ground and sat back against the slope, looking clear across to Convict Grade and the Crazy Mountains. I was blood from the elbows down. The antelope's eyes had skinned over. I thought: This is goddamned serious and you had better always remember that.

There was a big red enamel pot on the stove; and I ladled the antelope chili into two bowls for my son and me. He said, "It better not be too hot."

"It isn't."

"What's your news?" he asked.

"Grandpa's dead."

"Which grandpa?" he asked. I told him it was Big Grandpa, my father. He kept on eating. "He died last night." He said, "I know what I want for Christmas."

"What's that?"

"I want Big Grandpa back."

It was 1950-something and I was small, under twelve say, and there were four of us: my father, two of his friends, and me. There was a good belton setter belonging to the one friend, a hearty bird hunter who taught dancing and fist-fought at any provocation. The other man was old and sick and had a green fatal look in his face. My father took me aside and said, "Jack and I are going to the head of this field"—and he pointed up a mile and a half of stalks to where it ended in the flat woods—"and we're going to take the dog and get what he can point. These are running birds. So you and Bill just block the field and you'll have some shooting."

"I'd like to hunt with the dog." I had a 20-gauge Winchester my grandfather had given me, which got hocked and lost years later when another of my family got into the bottle; and I could hit with it and wanted to hunt over the setter. With respect to blocking the field, I could smell a rat.

"You stay with Bill," said my father, "and try to cheer him up."

"What's the matter with Bill?"

"He's had one heart attack after another and he's going to die."

"When?"

"Pretty damn soon."

I blocked the field with Bill. My first thought was, I hope he doesn't die before they drive those birds onto us; but if he does, I'll have all the shooting.

There was a crazy cold autumn light on everything, magnified by the yellow silage all over the field. The dog found birds right away and they were shooting. Bill said he was scary but he didn't feel so good. He had his hunting license safety pinned to the back of his coat and fiddled with a handful of 12-gauge shells. "I've shot a shitpile of game," said Bill, "but I don't feel so good anymore." He took a knife out of his coat pocket. "I got this in the Marines," he said, "and I carried it for four years in the Pacific. The handle's drilled out and weighted so you can throw it. I want you to have it." I took it and thanked him, looking into his green face, and wondered why he had given it to me. "That's for blocking this field with me," he said. "Your dad and that dance teacher are going to shoot them all. When you're not feeling so good, they put you at the end of the field to block when there isn't shit-all going to fly by you. They'll get them all. They and the dog will."

We had an indestructible tree in the yard we had chopped on, nailed steps to, and initialed; and when I pitched that throwing knife at it, the knife broke in two. I picked it up and thought: This thing is jinxed. So I took it out into the crabapple woods and put it in the can I had buried, along with a Roosevelt dime and an atomic-bomb ring I had sent away for. This was a small collection of things I buried over a period of years. I was sending them to God. All He had to do was open the can, but they were never collected. In any case, I have long known that if I could understand why I wanted to send a broken knife I believed to be jinxed to God, then I would be a long way toward what they call a personal philosophy as opposed to these hand-to-mouth metaphysics of who said what to whom in some cornfield twenty-five years ago.

We were in the bar at Chico Hot Springs near my home in Montana: me, a lout poet who had spent the day floating under the diving board while adolescent girls leapt overhead; and my brother John, who had glued himself to the pipe which poured warm water into the pool and announced over and over in a loud voice that every drop of water had been filtered through his bathing suit.

Now, covered with wrinkles, we were in the bar, talking to Alvin Close, an old government hunter. After half a century of predator control he called it "useless and half-assed."

Alvin Close killed the last major stock-killing wolf in Montana. He hunted the wolf so long he raised a litter of dogs to do it with. He hunted the wolf futilely with a pack that had fought the wolf a dozen times, until one day he gave up and let the dogs run the wolf out the back of a shallow canyon. He heard them yip their way into silence while he leaned up against a tree; and presently the wolf came tiptoeing down the front of the canyon into Alvin's lap. The wolf simply stopped because the game was up. Alvin raised the Winchester and shot it.

"How did you feel about that?" I asked.

"How do you think I felt?"

"I don't know."

"I felt like hell."

Alvin's evening was ruined and he went home. He was seventy-six years old and carried himself like an old-time army officer, setting his glass on the bar behind him without looking.

You stare through the plastic at the red smear of meat in the supermarket. What's this it says here? Mighty Good? Tastee? Quality, Premium, and Government Inspected? Soon enough, the blood is on your hands. It's inescapable.

Aldo Leopold was a hunter who I am sure abjured freeze-dried vegetables and extrusion burgers. His conscience was clean because his hunting was part of a larger husbandry in which the life of the country was enhanced by his own work.

He knew that game populations are not bothered by hunting until they are already precarious and that precarious game populations should not be hunted. Grizzlies should not be hunted, for instance. The enemy of game is clean farming and sinful chemicals; as well as the useless alteration of watersheds by promoter cretins and the insidious dizzards of land development, whose lobbyists teach us the venality of all governments.

A world in which a sacramental portion of food can be taken in an old way—hunting, fishing, farming, and gathering—has as much to do with societal sanity as a day's work for a day's pay.

For a long time, there was no tracking snow. I hunted on horseback for a couple of days in a complicated earthquake fault in the Gallatins. The fault made a maze of narrow canyons with flat floors. The sagebrush grew on woody trunks higher than my head and left sandy paths and game trails where the horse and I could travel.

There were Hungarian partridge that roared out in front of my horse, putting his head suddenly in my lap. And hawks tobogganed on the low air currents, astonished to find me there. One finger canyon ended in a vertical rock wall from which issued a spring of the kind elsewhere associated with the Virgin Mary, hung with ex-votos and the orthopedic supplications of satisfied miracle customers. Here, instead, were nine identical piles of bear shit, neatly adorned with undigested berries.

One canyon planed up and topped out on an endless grass rise. There were deer there; does and a young buck, a thousand yards away and staring at me with semaphore ears.

They assembled at a stiff trot from the haphazard array of feeding and strung out in a precise line against the far hill in a dogtrot. When I removed my hat, they went into their pogo-stick gait and that was that.

"What did a deer ever do to you?"

"Nothing."

"I'm serious. What do you have to go and kill them for?"

"I can't explain it talking like this."

"Why should they die for you? Would you die for deer?"

"If it came to that."

My boy and I went up the North Fork to look for grouse. We had my old pointer Molly, and Thomas's .22 pump. We flushed a number of birds climbing through the wild roses; but they roared away at knee level, leaving me little opportunity for my over-and-under, much less an opening for Thomas to ground-sluice one with his .22. We started out at the meteor hole above the last ranch and went all the way to the national forest. Thomas had his cap on the bridge of his nose and wobbled through the trees until we hit cross fences. We went out into the last open pasture before he got winded. So we sat down and looked across the valley at the Gallatin Range, furiously white and serrated, a bleak edge of the world. We sat in the sun and watched the chickadees make their way through the russet brush.

"Are you having a good time?"

"Sure," he said and curled a small hand around the

octagonal barrel of the Winchester. I was not sure what I had meant by my question.

The rear quarters of the antelope came from the smoker so dense and finely grained it should have been sliced as prosciutto. We had edgy, crumbling cheddar from British Columbia and everybody kept an eye on the food and tried to pace themselves. The snow whirled in the window light and puffed the smoke down the chimney around the cedar flames. I had a stretch of enumerating things: my family, hayfields, saddle horses, friends, thirty-aught six, French and Russian novels. I had a baby girl, colts coming, and a new roof on the barn. I finished a big corral made of railroad ties and two-by-sixes. I was within eighteen months of my father's death, my sister's death, and the collapse of my marriage. Still, the washouts were repairing; and when a few things had been set aside, not excluding paranoia, some features were left standing, not excluding lovers, children, friends, and saddle horses. In time, it would be clear as a bell. I did want venison again that winter and couldn't help but feel some old ridge-runner had my number on him.

I didn't want to read and I didn't want to write or acknowledge the phone with its tendrils into the zombie enclaves. I didn't want the New Rugged; I wanted the Old Rugged and a pot to piss in. Otherwise, it's deteriorata, with mice undermining the wiring in my frame house, sparks jumping in the insulation, the dog turning queer, and a horned owl staring at the baby through the nursery window.

It was pitch black in the bedroom and the windows radiated cold across the blankets. The top of my head felt this side of frost and the stars hung like ice crystals over the chimney. I scrambled out of bed and slipped into my long johns, put on a heavy shirt and my wool logger pants with the police suspenders. I carried the boots down to the kitchen so as not to wake the house and turned the percolator on. I put some cheese and chocolate in my coat, and when the coffee was done I filled a chili bowl and quaffed it against the winter.

When I hit the front steps I heard the hard squeaking of new snow under my boots and the wind moved against my face like a machine for refinishing hardwood floors. I backed the truck up to the horse trailer, the lights wheeling against the ghostly trunks of the bare cottonwoods. I connected the trailer and pulled it forward to a flat spot for loading the horse.

I had figured that when I got to the corral I could tell one horse from another by starlight; but the horses were in the shadow of the barn and I went in feeling my way among their shapes trying to find my hunting horse Rocky, and trying to get the front end of the big sorrel who kicks when surprised. Suddenly Rocky was looking in my face and I reached around his neck with the halter. A twelve-hundred-pound bay quarter horse, his withers angled up like a fighting bull, he wondered where we were going but ambled after me on a slack lead rope as we headed out of the darkened corral.

I have an old trailer made by a Texas horse vet years ago. It has none of the amenities of newer trailers. I wish it had a dome light for loading in the dark; but it doesn't. You ought to check and see if the cat's sleeping in it before you load; and

I didn't do that either. Instead, I climbed inside the trailer and the horse followed me. I tied the horse down to a D-ring and started back out, when he blew up. The two of us were confined in the small space and he was ripping and bucking between the walls with such noise and violence that I had a brief disassociated moment of suspension from fear. I jumped up on the manger with my arms around my head while the horse shattered the inside of the trailer and rocked it furiously on its axles. Then he blew the steel rings out of the halter and fell over backward in the snow. The cat darted out and was gone. I slipped down off the manger and looked for the horse; he had gotten up and was sidling down past the granary in the star shadows.

I put two blankets on him, saddled him, played with his feet, and calmed him. I loaded him without incident and headed out.

I went through the aspen line at daybreak, still climbing. The horse ascended steadily toward a high basin, creaking the saddle metronomically. It was getting colder as the sun came up, and the rifle scabbard held my left leg far enough from the horse that I was chilling on that side.

We touched the bottom of the basin and I could see the rock wall defined by a black stripe of evergreens on one side and the remains of an avalanche on the other. I thought how utterly desolate this country can look in winter and how one could hardly think of human travel in it at all, not white horsemen nor Indians dragging travois, just aerial raptors with their rending talons and heads like cameras slicing across the geometry of winter.

Then we stepped into a deep hole and the horse went to his chest in the powder, splashing the snow out before him as he floundered toward the other side. I got my feet out of the stirrups in case we went over. Then we were on wind-scoured rock and I hunted some lee for the two of us. I thought of my son's words after our last cold ride: "Dad, you know in 4-H? Well, I want to switch from Horsemanship to Aviation."

The spot was like this: a crest of snow crowned in a sculpted edge high enough to protect us. There was a tough little juniper to picket the horse to, and a good place to sit out of the cold and noise. Over my head, a long, curling plume of snow poured out, unchanging in shape against the pale blue sky. I ate some of the cheese and rewrapped it. I got the rifle down from the scabbard, loosened the cinch, and undid the flank cinch. I put the stirrup over the horn to remind me my saddle was loose, loaded two cartridges into the blind magazine, and slipped one in the chamber. Then I started toward the rock wall, staring at the patterned discolorations: old seeps, lichen, cracks, and the madhouse calligraphy of immemorial weather.

There were a lot of tracks where the snow had crusted out of the wind; all deer except for one well-used bobcat trail winding along the edges of a long rocky slot. I moved as carefully as I could, stretching my eyes as far out in front of my detectable movement as I could. I tried to work into the wind, but it turned erratically in the basin as the temperature of the new day changed.

The buck was studying me as soon as I came out on the open slope: he was a long way away and I stopped motionless to wait for him to feed again. He stared straight at me from five hundred yards. I waited until I could no longer feel my feet nor finally my legs. It was nearly an hour before he suddenly ducked his head and began to feed. Every time he fed I moved a few feet, but he was working away from me and I wasn't getting anywhere. Over the next half-hour he made his way to a little rim and, in the half-hour after that, moved the twenty feet that dropped him over the rim.

I went as fast as I could move quietly. I now had the rim to cover me and the buck should be less than a hundred yards from me when I looked over. It was all browse for a half-mile, wild roses, buck brush, and young quakies where there was any runoff.

When I reached the rim, I took off my hat and set it in the snow with my gloves inside. I wanted to be looking in the right direction when I cleared the rim, rise a half step and be looking straight at the buck, not scanning for the buck with him running sixty, a degree or two out of my periphery. And I didn't want to gum it up with thinking or trajectory guessing. People are always trajectory guessing their way into gut shots and clean misses. So, before I took the last step, all there was to do was lower the rim with my feet, lower the buck into my vision, and isolate the path of the bullet.

As I took that step, I knew he was running. He wasn't in the browse at all, but angling into invisibility at the rock wall, racing straight into the elevation, bounding toward zero gravity, taking his longest arc into the bullet and the finality and terror of all you have made of the world, the finality you know that you share even with your babies with their inherited and ambiguous dentition, the finality that any minute now you will meet as well.

He slid a hundred yards in a rush of snow. I dressed him and skidded him by one antler to the horse. I made a slit behind the last ribs, pulled him over the saddle and put the horn through the slit, lashed the feet to the cinch dees, and led the horse downhill. The horse had bells of clear ice around his hoofs, and when he slipped, I chipped them out from under his feet with the point of a bullet.

I hung the buck in the open woodshed with a lariat over a rafter. He turned slowly against the cooling air. I could see the intermittent blue light of the television against the bedroom ceiling from where I stood. I stopped the twirling of the buck, my hands deep in the sage-scented fur, and thought: This is either the beginning or the end of everything.

A herd of fleeing antelope skimming over the plain, wheeling, maneuvering, is like nothing so much as a flock of swallows.

—JACK O'CONNOR

In one's imagination one might still look out over the vast, rolling, open vistas of this wheat country and see the shortgrass prairie before the arrival of the sodbuster, might imagine the buffalo herds and the Plains Indian tribes and the sheer wild immensity of country.

—JIM FERGUS

Hunters fresh from urbania seldom see an animal unless it's standing in the open . . . Over the years I've trained myself to look for a turn of horn, a section of haunch, an unusual profile, a shadow, a color out of place, a difference in texture.

—TOM WALKER

To hunt means to have the land around you like clothing. To engage in a wordless dialogue with it, one so absorbing that you cease to talk with your human companions.

—BARRY LOPEZ

What is the apex of the hunt? At what point is the bond between pursuer and prey finally, firmly sealed? Is it the hunter's departure from the community into the wilderness? The first sighting of the animal? The aim? Is it the moment the hunter touches the still-warm flesh and considers the feast? Maybe the hunt never ends at all, but keeps circling back to where it started, each phase completing its own perfect orbit, and all of them together forming the cycle of life and death, hunger and fulfillment, like the parts of a great clock that strikes only at midnight every hundred years, and that striking is the apex of the hunt.

—Trebbe Johnson

As late as the end of the seventeenth century the turbulent village nobles of Lithuania and Livonia hunted the bear, the bison, the elk, the wolf, and the stag, and hung the spoils in their smoky wooden palaces; and so, two hundred years later, the free hunters of Montana, in the interludes between hazardous mining guests and bloody Indian campaigns, hunted game almost or quite the same kind, through the cold mountain forests surrounding the Yellowstone and Flathead lakes, and decked their log cabins and ranch houses with the hides and horns of the slaughtered beasts.

—Theodore Roosevelt

Two roads diverged in a wood, and I—
I took the one less traveled by,
And that has made all the difference."

—ROBERT FROST

. . .The essence of life is that it lives by killing and eating, that's the great mystery . . . the basic hunting myth is a kind of covenant between the animal world and the human world.

—JOSEPH CAMPBELL

*Of course in hunting one must expect much hardship
and repeated disappointment; and in many a
camp, bad weather, lack of shelter, hunger, thirst,
or ill success with game, renders the days and nights
irksome and trying. Yet the hunter worthy of the
name always willingly takes the bitter if by so
doing he can get the sweet, and gladly balances
failure and success, spurning the poorer souls who
know neither.*

—THEODORE ROOSEVELT

In my freezer there's the meat of an elk, the being whom I consider the distillate of this country… When thawed he smells faintly of what he ate last summer: grass and sedge, wildflowers, stream water. He smells of this place, which, when I eat him, becomes an inholding within me… We have joined and it's the hunting that creates the conjunction.

—TED KERASOTE

*Caribou meat isn't as sweet as that of an elk.
They're not as cagey as a whitetail. You wouldn't
call them dangerous. But jeez, look at that rack!"*

—Don Robertson

. . .The call of the bulls. . . heard in the depths of
their own mountain fastnesses, ringing through the
frosty night, and echoing across the ravines and
under the silent archways of the pines, it has a
grand, musical beauty of its own . . .

—THEODORE ROOSEVELT

... When others attempt to impose their attitudes,
values and tastes on my leisure pursuits ... when
they attempt to dictate my diet ... when they sully
and portray the choice of hunting as immoral ...
then the abridgment of morality has not been
committed by me, but by my accusers.

—MATTHEW B. CONNOLLY, JR.

It is wonderful how cozy a camp, in clear weather, becomes if there is a good fire and enough to eat, and how sound the sleep is afterward in the cool air, with the brilliant stars glimmering through the branches overhead.

—THEODORE ROOSEVELT

Most of the paint was worn off the wings and the propeller looked out of kilter. I'm not sure, but the pontoons seemed to be taking-in water, and visions of the Hindenburg, Titanic, and Amelia Earhart were flying through my brain. I'd never seen a cropduster as old as this, and I wouldn't think of riding a bicycle in this condition. After 14 days without a shower, though, I looked at my partner and asked, "Front seat or back?

—THOMAS ROBERTS

If the sentimentalist were right, hunting would develop in men a cruelty of character. But I have found that it inculcates patience, demands discipline and iron nerve, and develops a serenity of spirit that makes for long life and long love of life.

—Archibald Rutledge

...In all this wide lovely country, in all these diverse climates, birds and animals live and move, find their own food, escape their enemies, love briefly and violently like the deer or long and tenderly like the quail, guard and cherish their young, and finally die, usually horribly, for Nature, lovely though she is, has no love for the awkward, the slow, the old and the weak.

—JACK O'CONNOR

Elk hunting runs deep. Not that it's always fun, because it isn't. It's a contrast in superlatives, ranging from agony to euphoria, and it will stretch your sense and your senses to the limit . . . It raises you higher, drops you lower, subjects you to conditions that penetrate deep into your body, mind, emotions, and soul. You may like elk hunting, you may not, but definitely you won't forget it.

—DWIGHT SCHUH

'Seeing the elephant' is the realization of man's smallness and inadequacy in a large, wild place. It is the realization that, to the elemental forces that make mountains, a human life is no more (nor less) valued than that of an elk, a mouse, or a fungus. We may kill and eat the elk. The mouse may eat the mushroom. But someday, a fungus will eat what remains of elk, mouse, and man.

—AARON FRASER PASS